ADELE JOHNSTON

MANAGING RELATIONSHIPS

A Teen's Handbook for Love, Dating & Heartbreak

MANAGING RELATIONSHIPS

A Teen's Handbook for Love, Dating & Heartbreak

ADELE JOHNSTON

Note from the author:

I want to acknowledge and respect the diverse experiences and identities of individuals, including gender and sexuality. However, for the clarity and simplicity in this text, I will be using gender-specific language such as 'boyfriend,' 'girlfriend,' 'him,' 'her,' etc. This choice is not to diminish or exclude anyone, but rather to align with the context and purpose of this book.

Dedication

To all the students who have opened their hearts and shared their stories with me about love and loss – you are my heroes. Your courage, vulnerability and honesty have shaped many of the words in these pages. This book is for you.

Published in 2025 by Amba Press, Melbourne, Australia
www.ambapress.com.au

© Adele Johnston 2025

All rights reserved. No part of this book may be reproduced or transmitted in any form or by any means, electronic or mechanical, including photocopying, recording or by any information storage and retrieval system, without prior permission in writing from the publisher.

Cover design: Tess McCabe
Internal design: Midlands
Editor: Rica Dearman

ISBN: 9781923215887 (pbk)
ISBN: 9781923215894 (ebk)

A catalogue record for this book is available from the National Library of Australia.

Contents

Introduction 1

Part one   Self-love
Chapter 1   How to be OK being on your own   5
Chapter 2   How to get to know yourself   11
Chapter 3   How to accept yourself   17
Chapter 4   How to take care of yourself   25
Chapter 5   How to know if you're ready for a relationship   29

Part two   Dating and relationships
Chapter 6   How to date   37
Chapter 7   How to be in a relationship   53

Part three   Heartbreak and rejection
Chapter 8   How to deliver and handle a break-up   63
Chapter 9   How to cope after a break-up   71

Conclusion   81
References   83

Introduction

Are you:

- Keen to grow more confidence?
- Single but want to be in a relationship?
- Crushing on someone but don't know how to ask them out?
- In a 'situationship' but want more commitment?
- In a new relationship and want to keep improving it?
- In a relationship but don't feel secure?
- In a relationship but struggling to communicate your needs?
- In a relationship but not sure if you should stay or go?
- Broken-hearted or recently rejected?

Using practical strategies and a dash of science, this book will try to help you to feel more confident and in control of your love life.

PART ONE
Self-love

CHAPTER 1

How to be OK being on your own

Why is it important to love yourself?

Movies and songs are full of messages about the importance of loving ourselves:

- 'Special' – Lizzo
- 'I Love Me' – Meghan Trainor
- 'My mind is a warrior' – Ed Sheeran
- 'If there is one thing I'm willing to bet on, it's myself' – Beyoncé
- 'I didn't want to join a band, so I started my own' – Spider-Man
- 'Learn to ignore the names people call you and just trust who you are' – Shrek
- 'Love yourself and you're set. I'm on the right track, baby I was born this way' – Lady Gaga
- 'I'm bejewelled. When I walk in the room. I can still make the whole place shimmer' – Taylor Swift

So, why do people like Lizzo and Meghan Trainor think it's so important to love yourself? Let me explain through a story...

Sarah and John were inseparable in high school. They would spend every lunchtime together and hang out on weekends. They moved in together when they started university and relied on each other for everything. They built a cocoon of comfort around each other. Five years after they moved in together, John blindsided Sarah by telling her he no longer wanted to be with her. Sarah was a mess. She didn't know how to cope without him. She didn't know what she wanted or needed. She hated the feeling of being alone and didn't have any friends to turn to because she had always put John first. Being by herself became so uncomfortable that she jumped into another relationship with the first guy who showed her any interest.

Do you think Sarah got her 'happily ever after'? Do you think she would have handled her break-up differently if she'd had more understanding and confidence in herself and what she wanted?

Life is full of hard times: friends can be mean, our parents can get divorced, we can fail exams, we can have serious health issues or learning difficulties, our loved ones can die, crushes can ghost us. How do we get through these difficult times? We can't always rely on our friends, teachers, parents or partners to protect us. We have to learn to fend for ourselves and draw on our strengths to get through these hard times.

One of the ways we can 'fend for ourselves' is to learn to love ourselves. This is one of the most important life lessons you will learn, because it helps you to respect yourself and work out what you need. So, when the 'love of your life' comes along, you won't have to rely on them to make you happy; because in the words of Lizzo, you know, 'I'm gon' be OK', and you won't fall apart if things don't work out.

What gets in the way of loving yourself?

Loving ourselves is not always easy. One of the reasons for this is because our brains are hardwired to focus on 'what's wrong' rather than 'what's strong'. We tend to focus on the negatives because it's what saved us from being pounced on, stung or chased by predators back in the cave era. But today our lives aren't at risk 24/7, so we have to consciously train our brains to also look for the good.

Here are some factors that can hold us back from achieving self-love:

Negative self-talk

Criticising ourselves by saying things like 'I'm useless', 'I'm ugly', 'no one will ever love me' and 'it's all my fault' is the opposite of self-love because we are only focusing on our flaws and mistakes. On the other hand, self-love involves acceptance, forgiveness and kindness towards ourselves.

Comparison

Comparing ourselves to others is a biological part of being human because it helps us to figure out how we measure up to others. But, thanks to social media bombarding us with 'picture-perfect' lives, comparing ourselves to others can quickly become toxic and put our self-love at risk.

Societal messages

We are flooded with societal messages that tell us that in order to be successful, we need to obtain high academic results in school, complete a university degree, find a partner, establish a good career, get married and have kids. But what if we haven't managed to achieve some of these goals at the same time as our friends or we choose to take a different path? This messaging can be a constant reminder that 'we haven't made it' or we are 'not there yet', which can negatively impact our self-love and make us feel like failures.

What are some signs you don't love yourself enough?

- You don't take care of your body.
- You put more energy into pleasing others than yourself.
- You apologise for everything.
- You blame yourself for everything.
- You treat others unkindly.
- You put yourself down.
- You feel guilty when you take time out for yourself.
- You surround yourself with toxic people.
- You beat yourself up over your past mistakes and failures.
- You second-guess yourself and struggle to trust your own 'gut feeling'.

What are the benefits of loving yourself?

- Better sleep
- Less anxious
- More determined
- More motivated
- Higher self-esteem
- Increased self-awareness
- More self-acceptance
- Less stress

What are the advantages of being single?

Have you ever worried about being single? Maybe your friends are in relationships and you feel left out. Maybe you have been single for a while and fear that you might be alone forever.

There is a lot of negative stigma around being single, thanks to long-held societal standards that having a partner, buying a home and having kids lead to a happy life. But at your age, there is plenty of time for those things! Your focus should be on getting to know yourself and having as many interesting life experiences as possible.

In one study that focused on the question 'what makes single life attractive?', participants appreciated the following:

- No one tells me what to do and I don't have to explain myself to anyone.
- I don't have to worry about getting hurt, rejected, cheated on or jealous.
- I can focus on my goals and have more time to focus on my studies and career.
- I have more freedom to 'flirt around'.
- I have more time to myself to do the things I enjoy.
- I have more time to invest in my friends.

CHAPTER 2

How to get to know yourself

What is self-awareness?

Have you ever taken the time to ask yourself 'who am I?'

What are your values? Passions? Aspirations? Are you aware of your thoughts? Feelings? Behaviours? What are your strengths and weaknesses?

Self-awareness is about having a clear understanding of your true self; why you feel and behave in certain ways.

Your path towards self-awareness is one of the most important journeys you will ever take because it will empower you to create the life you want.

How to recognise the emotions you are feeling

Throughout high school and beyond, lots of different emotions are going to come up for you.

There are going to be times when you feel…

- *Tired* because you stayed up too late writing assignments
- *Panicked* because you haven't started your assignment and it's due tomorrow
- *Excited* because you just had your first kiss
- *Scared* because you don't want to say the wrong thing around your friends
- *Confused* when you don't know where you stand with a crush
- *Proud* because you passed your exams
- *Angry* because someone has let you down
- *Joyful* when a new relationship begins
- *Heartbroken* when a relationship ends
- *Overwhelmed* as you try to balance study, part-time work and a social life

When you feel some of these emotions, do you face them, feel them and process them? Or do you run from them, avoid them and distract yourself?

Emotions are just signals that tell us we need to pay attention to what's going on within and around us so our life can continue to run smoothly.

Sitting with and facing our unpleasant feelings head-on is uncomfortable, but it's more helpful in the long run because it allows us to move forward more productively. When we bury our feelings, they build up inside us, prolonging our pain, or they might eventually explode causing destruction to those around us.

How to deal with your emotions

- Recognise where you feel the emotion in your body (head, heart, chest, stomach…).
- Label the emotion – 'I'm feeling angry', 'I'm feeling embarrassed', 'I'm feeling sad'.
- Accept that the emotion is here and talk to yourself like you would to a friend: 'I am OK', 'I did my best', 'this will pass'.
- Remind yourself that emotions don't last if we let them come and let them go without 'adding on' to the emotion with judgements and stories that aren't true.
- Ask yourself: 'What is in my control and what is not in my control?'
- Calm yourself by:
  - Breathing
  - Moving (walking, running, yoga)
  - Crying
  - Talking to a friend
- Write down how you are feeling (writing by hand slows down our thinking and forces us to be more present to stay with our thoughts and helps us to process and clarify thoughts and feelings).
- Once you have calmed yourself, reflect by asking questions to help you gain perspective and empathy around your situation:
  - What caused me to feel this way?
  - Was it a result of my critical thoughts or something someone else did or said?
  - Is this a pattern that keeps happening?

Don't believe everything your thoughts tell you

Imagine that you tell one of your closest friends that you have feelings for them, and they tell you they don't feel the same. You feel rejected, embarrassed and fearful that you have destroyed your friendship. How do you talk to yourself when you are experiencing these tough emotions? Do you speak to yourself like you would to a friend and say, 'that must really hurt', 'you should be proud for being brave and taking the risk'. Or do you say, 'I'm an idiot', 'of course they don't like me', 'I'm ugly', 'I've ruined everything'.

As I've already mentioned, when we experience a difficult situation, our thoughts tend to sway towards the negative, so we need to be mindful and question our thoughts because they love to make up stories that can make us feel even worse.

Just because your thoughts tell you something doesn't mean it's true. Your thoughts are just thoughts. They are not facts. According to psychologist Michael Stein, "If you take everything your mind says seriously, give it too much respect and put too much trust in your thoughts, that is a recipe for an anxiety disorder." The healthier way to approach your thoughts is not to take them so seriously. Don't believe everything your thoughts tell you. They are not facts.

How to be the boss of your negative self-talk

1. Recognise what you are saying to yourself

The next time you feel stressed, angry, scared or sad, stop what you are doing and take a few deep breaths and notice or write down what your thoughts are saying to you. The more you practise recognising your thoughts, the better you can get at catching them before they get out of control.

2. Challenge your thoughts

Be a detective and ask yourself, 'is this thought true?', 'is it a fact?' Get curious and ask yourself, 'is there another way of looking at this situation or another explanation?'

3. Ask: 'is this thought helpful?'

According to Dr Russ Harris (author of *The Happiness Trap*), rather than spending energy working out if your thoughts are true or false, it's more beneficial to ask whether your thoughts are helpful and whether they are helping you to create the life you want to lead. The next time you notice your negative thoughts, ask yourself, 'what could be a more helpful thought?'

4. Name your 'negative self-talk' with something comical

Naming your 'inner critic' with something comical, like evil characters from Disney movies such as, 'Cruella' or 'Scar', can help take away your thought's power. The next time you hear 'Cruella' tell you, 'no wonder she dumped you', 'everyone thinks I'm weird', simply say, 'there's Cruella again' or 'here comes Cruella again', then just let it be. You don't have to challenge her or push her away or give her much attention. Let her come and go and channel your energy into doing something you value, like hanging out with your friends or going for a run.

CHAPTER 3

How to accept yourself

What is self-acceptance?

Self-acceptance is about knowing your strengths, weaknesses and values. It's about fully accepting and being at peace with who you are, knowing that you are never going to please everyone, and that nobody is perfect.

When you fully accept yourself, it can protect you from judging yourself too harshly and help you to release things you can't control.

What are your strengths?

Part of learning to accept yourself is knowing your strengths.

Most of us can easily identify our weaknesses because, as I mentioned at the beginning of this book, we are hardwired to focus on the negative. Consequently, we have to intentionally encourage our brains to focus on our strengths.

✏ Journal Time

1. What frequent compliments do people give you? For example, 'you are kind', 'you are brave'.

2. If you were to choose five strengths from the list below that you use on a regular basis, which ones would you choose?

If you want to be more accurate, I suggest doing the 15-minute VIA Character Strengths Survey (found at www.viacharacter.org) and find out your 24 strengths in order.

3. After you complete the VIA Character Strengths Survey, have a look at your top five strengths. Do they feel like you? Do they feel authentic to who you are? Why? Why not?

How can you use your strengths to build self-acceptance?

Here are some exercises you can work through to learn more about your strengths...

1. Write down a summary of one of your happiest or proudest moments. What strengths were you using throughout this moment?

2. What is something you are struggling with at the moment? How can you use your top five strengths to help you tackle this problem?

3. Can you think of a time you have used some of your lower strengths?

4. List one 'relationship' goal, for example, I want to make more friends, I want to ask someone to be more than just friends. How can you use your top five strengths to help you achieve that goal?

How to improve your weaknesses

Despite what you may see on social media every day, no one is perfect. We all have our weak points. While it's more important to focus on building our strengths because they are what make us feel energised and more engaged in what we do, it's still important to acknowledge and accept our weaknesses.

Another way of describing our weaknesses is the 'overuse or underuse of our strengths'.

For example, the overuse of *curiosity* could look like asking a new student who comes to your school a million questions; this could come across as being nosy. The underuse of *fairness* could mean that you don't stand up for yourself if your boyfriend/girlfriend blames you for not making enough time to hang out because you have been studying a lot. The overuse of *love* could look like smothering your partner with too much attention. The underuse of *humour* could come across as being too serious. The overuse of *perseverance* could look like not knowing when to quit and burning out.

✏️ Journal Time

Underuse

1. Think of a time you underused a strength. How can you become more aware of this strength? In what situations could you use it more often?

Overuse

2. Think of a time you overused a strength. How could you dial it down next time? What's another strength you could use to balance the other strength out?

How to be more kind to yourself when you have failed

How do you treat yourself when you fail a test, get rejected by your crush or get caught talking behind a friend's back?

Self-compassion is about giving ourselves encouragement and support instead of being mean and self-judgemental when we go through hard times.

✏ Journal Time

Tips to build self-compassion

1. **What would a friend say to you?**

   What would one of your closest friends say to you when you are being too hard on yourself?

2. **Positive affirmations**

   Make a poster of these affirmations and stick them somewhere you will see them regularly or write them on a sticky note and say them over and over to yourself when you have made a mistake.

   - I am allowed to make mistakes, and I forgive myself.
   - I accept my faults because nobody is perfect.
   - Mistakes show that I am learning and growing.
   - I won't let my negative self-talk hold me back.
   - I did the best I could.

3. **Journal prompts**

   Writing down our thoughts helps us cope with stressful events because it can help us to distance ourselves from a situation and make sense of what happened. You can buy great journals from Kikki.K or just get a plain notebook from your nearest newsagent. Here are some journal prompts to try:

   What was happening in the moment?

   - I felt sad/frustrated/angry because of…
   - Looking back when… happened, I wasn't thinking clearly and now I feel embarrassed/regretful/silly.
   - I can see that my reaction or what I did was caused by feelings of fear/guilt/impatience…

   Everyone makes mistakes

   - Everyone feels anxious/confused/cranky…
   - It was a complex situation. Most people would also find it difficult to handle.
   - We all lose our self-control occasionally. No one is perfect.

   Self-kindness

   - I forgive myself for feeling sad/overwhelmed/hurt…
   - I made a mistake and lost my temper/turned up late/said something mean about a friend and that's OK. Next time I will…
   - There is no point dwelling on it. It's done. Tomorrow I will…

4. **What can I do to look after myself now?**

   Choose three of these self-care activities to try:

   - Go for a walk.
   - Talk to a friend.
   - Have a long shower.
   - Read a book.
   - Tidy your room.
   - Take a nap.
   - Make your favourite meal.
   - Listen to a meditation.
   - Listen to your favourite playlist.
   - Watch your favourite Netflix series.
   - Write a list of things you are grateful for.
   - Listen to an audio book or podcast.
   - Plan something fun to do with friends or family on the weekend.
   - Go to bed early.
   - Sleep in.

   Do you have anything else you like to do to take care of yourself when you are feeling down?

CHAPTER 4

How to take care of yourself

When we trip over and scratch our knee or fall off a bike, we take care of ourselves by putting a Band-Aid on the wound, so it doesn't get infected.

But how do you take care of yourself when you are suffering emotionally or mentally? How do you take care of yourself when you are feeling heartbroken, lonely, rejected or embarrassed?

Our wellbeing is made up of more than just physical health. Here are six strategies that researchers recommend to enhance positive emotions, engagement, relationships, meaning, accomplishment and health.

✏ Journal Time

1. Look for the good

What is good in your life at the moment?

I know you have heard this a million times, but practising gratitude really does make us feel good and strengthens our relationships.

Admittedly, it's much harder to hunt for the good when you are feeling down. But it's important that you try to find something to be grateful for at least once a week, because your brain needs to get a hit of positive hormones to make you feel better. Looking for the good doesn't have to be time-consuming. For example, every night before you go to sleep you could ask yourself, 'what was the best part of my day?'

2. Minimise distractions

What is one activity you love doing where you feel 'in the zone', where you are totally absorbed in what you are doing and you don't notice time passing you by?

When we experience 'flow' our mind doesn't wander. We don't worry about our problems, and we are completely focused on the task.

What gets in the way of you being 'in the zone'? For example, distractions such as your phone buzzing, the sound of the television or radio, your friends or family interrupting you?

What could you do to minimise those distractions so you can find more moments to focus on the things that energise you?

3. Ask for help

Top performers and successful people do not reach success on their own. Ash Barty's 'support crew', for example, consisted of her tennis coach, her strength and conditioning coach, her mindset coach, her physio, her partner, her family and friends; she never operated alone and attributes her success to her team.

And yet we often try to handle problems on our own.

Researchers claim that when we are feeling low, reaching out to someone else will give us the quickest boost to our wellbeing.

Write a list of your 'support crew' that you can reach out to when you need some help, for example, mother, father, auntie, friends, guidance counsellor.

4. Spend time alone

While being around others is important for our wellbeing, finding alone time is also crucial because it allows us to regulate our emotions and reflect on things that have happened in the past or things that might occur in the future. It helps us to solve problems and think about what might have caused them.

It helps us to get to know ourselves, learn new things and develop our creative skills.

We can spend time alone by simply sitting outside or going for a walk, run or bike ride.

How can you build some alone time into your day?

5. Get involved

Get involved in activities, hobbies or sports outside of your school schedule. It could be learning a new language, attending art classes, playing sports, performing in a play or debating.

You are more likely to do better in your studies if you make time for leisure and recreation. Plus, it's a great way to meet new people and expand your friendship circle.

What are some hobbies, sports or extracurricular activities you have always wanted to try?

When will you commit to participating in these activities?

6. Make sleep a priority

Research suggests that teenagers need 8-10 hours of sleep every night, but many are only getting 6-7, which may cause chronic sleep deprivation. Lack of sleep can lead to relationship problems, poor grades and health problems like heart disease, obesity and depression.

So, how can you improve your sleep?

Here are three tips from sleep expert Matthew Walker:

- **Regularity** – go to bed at the same time and wake up at the same time no matter if it's a weekday or the weekend.

- **Keep it cool** – our bodies need to drop our core temperature 1-2°C to be able to initiate sleep and stay asleep. Make sure you have a fan or aircon to keep your room cool.

- **Get out of bed if you can't sleep** – the reason for this is if you don't, then your brain will quickly associate your bed with a place of being awake, so you need to break that association. Read a book or listen to an audio book, sleep story or meditation (stay off your phone as the blue light will keep you awake). Only return to bed when you are sleepy.

What's getting in the way of you sleeping 8-10 hours a night? What do you need to change?

CHAPTER 5

How to know if you're ready for a relationship

We've talked about the importance of loving yourself first, the next question to ask yourself is…

Why do you want to be in a relationship?

Is it because:

- All your friends are in relationships and you feel left out?
- Your friends are pressuring you to be in a relationship?
- You're trying to fit in with a new group of friends?
- You're trying to prove something to your parents?
- You're lonely?
- You feel that having a boyfriend/girlfriend will improve your confidence?

These are not good reasons to get into a relationship. Remember, it's OK to be single even if your friends are in relationships.

Here are some healthy reasons you might want to be in a relationship:

- You are attracted to someone and are comfortable with who you are.
- It's what you want, not what you think you should have.
- You are prepared to wait for the right person.
- It's your choice to be in a relationship and you're not being pressured by others.

What is your relationship vision?

After hooking up with several guys that treated her poorly and weren't giving her the relationship she wanted, Maddy decided she needed to change tactics. She couldn't control how others treated her, but she could control who she chose to let into her life. She wrote down a vision for the type of person and relationship she wanted. She also wrote down her 'deal breakers' – the things that would make her speak up in or end a relationship. Once she got clear on what she wanted, she started attracting more of the 'right guys' into her life.

Dave was in Year 12 and was feeling stressed because he was the only one out of his friendship group who was yet to find a formal partner. Eventually, he got set up with a girl called Linda from another school. Dave and Linda started Snapchatting and met for the first time at pre-formal drinks. Dave thought Linda was a nice girl and while he wasn't overly attracted to her and found her personality a bit bland, he thought he would ask her out again because he didn't want to be the only one in his group without a girlfriend. Dave ended up staying with Linda for a couple of years after high school, but he was never satisfied or happy in the relationship because he just 'fell into' it.

Most people are like Dave. They float aimlessly through life letting other people pull them in the direction they want to go instead of being intentional. In the words of Henry Kissinger, "If you don't know where you are going, every road will get you nowhere."

If you don't take the time to get clear on who you are and what you want in a relationship, you will always be settling for less. When you do this, you devalue yourself and convince yourself that you aren't worthy of an extraordinary relationship.

Like Maddy, it's important to experiment and date different people, but the sooner you can get clear on what you want, the less time you will waste on the wrong person.

Choosing your 'life partner' is one of the most important decisions you will ever make. I know you are not there yet, but it's valuable to think about it now because your partner has the potential to bring you great happiness or great misery.

Here are some exercises to help you get clear on finding a great relationship.

✏ Journal Time

How do you want to feel in a relationship?

In the table below, circle or list five emotions in your journal that you want to feel when you are in a relationship.

Accepted	Inspired	Present	Secure	Peaceful
Calm	Lively	Relaxed	Worthy	Energised
Content	Passionate	Trusting	Interested	Excited
Fulfilled	Playful	Alive	Sexy	Free
Patient	Vibrant	Joyful	Loved	Happy
Safe	Confident	Strong		

In the early stages of dating, ask yourself, 'does this person make me feel these emotions?'

Have you ever been or are currently in a relationship that makes you feel any of the following emotions?

Embarrassed	Ashamed	Humiliated	Worthless	Upset
Self-conscious	Fearful	Weak	Trapped	Irritated
	Afraid	Nervous	Edgy	Rejected
Useless	Anxious	Scared	Moody	Unsure
Depressed	Frightened	Worried	Sad	Powerless
Hesitant	Hopeless			

If so, you might want to reflect on whether this is the right relationship for you.

Characteristics of a healthy relationship

Here are some characteristics that you might look for in a healthy relationship. Tick the ones that stand out as being the most important to you:

- You can tell them anything and not feel judged.
- You feel safe and secure even when you are not with them because they are a good communicator.
- They are happy to hang out with your friends and family, but also let you hang out with them on your own.
- They give you space when you want to be alone.
- They support all the activities you love doing outside of school.
- They have their own hobbies and interests.
- They ask you for your advice and opinion.
- They accept that you can both have different opinions and viewpoints.
- They are a good listener.
- They can say 'I'm sorry' and they can also accept your apology.
- You can have healthy arguments with them that don't involve them putting you down.
- They support your goals and compliment you on your strengths.
- They treat their family, friends and strangers with respect.
- They don't get jealous of your male/female friends.

Must-haves, nice-to-haves and won't-haves

Must-haves	Nice-to-haves	Won't-haves
Write a 'wish list' of all the qualities (physical and emotional) you MUST have in a partner. Be as specific as you can and don't judge yourself for being 'too picky'. This is your chance to write down everything you truly want. **For example:** • They are kind to their parents, friends, teachers, strangers. • They are motivated and work hard. They are not lazy. • They look after their bodies by exercising and playing sport.	Write a list of all the qualities that would be nice to have but are not deal-breakers. **For example:** • They have a good sense of humour. • They work hard and want to do well in school. • They are taller/shorter than you. • They enjoy similar hobbies.	Write a list of all the qualities and behaviours you will not tolerate and put up with. **For example:** • Someone who takes drugs. • Someone who doesn't make plans with you. • Someone who is rude to strangers. • Someone who lies.

PART TWO
Dating and relationships

CHAPTER 6

How to date

How do you meet someone?

Most of you will meet your love interests in school, online, through sports, family friends, hobbies or a part-time job.

The key to making new connections is putting yourself out there to widen your network and taking the initiative. Get involved in the school musical, play a sport, join the debating team or do whatever floats your boat outside of your regular classes.

If you meet someone you 'click' with, ask for their number or if you can add them as a friend on social media. Don't be afraid to make the first move; someone always has to go first. The more you practise going first, the easier it will get and the more confident you will be. Communication is key when you are getting to know someone.

Here is a list of what good communication looks like:

- Use direct eye contact (it helps to build stronger social bonds).
- Smile.
- Use their name.
- Ask questions (about their family, their sports, hobbies, subjects, teachers, their future goals).
- Listen (repeat back what they have said).
- Don't interrupt.
- Be willing to be vulnerable and share honest parts about yourself (I know this can be scary, but it will deepen your relationship).

Defining your relationship – what are we?

So, you've met someone you 'click' with; now what?

It depends on what you want.

Go back to your relationship vision. What are you looking for? It's OK if you don't know yet. Here are some things to consider that might help you gain some clarity.

Do you want something casual?

A casual relationship, otherwise known as a 'booty call', 'hook-up', 'friend with benefits' is a more relaxed physical and emotional relationship that involves 'no strings attached' or no commitment. They are not long term and usually have an 'expiry date'. They allow you the freedom to date and sleep with other people.

Clear communication is key in a casual relationship

A casual relationship is not clearcut and can mean different things to different people. Therefore, it's important that if this is what you want, you need to communicate this very clearly at the start to avoid any confusion.

For example, Amy might think that a casual relationship involves having sleepovers and hanging out in public occasionally, but Josh might think that a casual relationship only involves sleepovers with no public appearances.

Sarah might think that a casual relationship means you don't have to reply to a message for a few days, but Dan might think that it involves continuous back and forth communication.

If you are someone who likes to plan, coordinate and organise, then you might prefer to date exclusively.

Advantages of casual relationships

1. They're good practice for the 'real thing'
You can practise your communication skills and make mistakes that will help you to do better in your future relationships.

2. They're fun
You get to connect with a variety of new people and share new experiences.

3. They give you time to focus on yourself
You can spend more time doing the things you love and focusing on your own growth without having to make compromises.

Disadvantages of casual relationships

1. You might fall for them

When you spend a lot of time with someone, you can risk growing a crush that isn't so casual.

2. You have to have low expectations

You can't rely on a casual partner to pick you up when you are feeling down or stay by your side all night at a party or hang out with you and your family on a regular basis. Casual relationships are meant to be 'easy breezy', light and fun. This might cause you to resent the person because you don't feel emotionally supported.

3. You might get jealous

Depending on the 'rules' you set for your relationship, if you have agreed that you are allowed to see other people, this might cause you to feel jealous, which is not a healthy situation to be in.

Do you want something more exclusive?

Dating someone exclusively means you have agreed not to see or sleep with anyone else. It's when you spend time doing fun activities together, such as going to the movies, having picnics in the park, bike riding or trips to the beach, etc. Exclusive dating is an opportunity to see if there is a potential for a long-term relationship.

Advantages of exclusive dating

1. Develop a deeper connection

You can focus on getting to know one person without any other distractions.

2. Provides a 'middle ground'

Exclusive dating allows you to sit in the middle between casual dating and a serious relationship. It gives you time and space to work out if you are a good match.

3. Gives you more stability

You are clearer about where you stand because you have mutually decided not to see anyone else. You have more assurance and can focus on whether your relationship has long-term potential.

Disadvantages of exclusive dating

1. You might get FOMO

You might experience FOMO about missing out on other relationships.

2. It might not work out

When you spend a lot of time with one person, it's natural that your connection gets deeper. This can make it more painful if things don't work out.

3. Different timelines

We all have different timelines. One person might want to take their time getting to know you, but the other person might already know they want to be with you. This can create pressure to decide whether to fully commit, keep dating or part ways.

When should you have sex?

There is no 'right' answer to this question. Deciding when to have sex is a personal choice, but it's worth noting that the legal age for sex in Australia is 16 or 17 depending on your state. Sex is a very intimate thing to do with someone. It involves a high level of trust and communication that is important for both people to feel safe.

Why wait?

There is a lot of research that says sex before 16 is linked to negative outcomes such as:

- Higher risk of sexually transmitted infections (STIs)
- Increased possibility of having sex when drunk (and regretting it)
- Higher chance of unwanted pregnancy
- Higher chance of abuse
- Higher rate of depression and anxiety

Not the best reasons to have sex:

- You want someone to like you.
- You're the only virgin in your group.
- Your boyfriend/girlfriend said they would break up with you if you don't have sex.
- You want to 'get it over with'.
- Having sex will make you more popular.

Am I ready questions:

- Why do I want to have sex?
- Does my reason align with my values?
- Is it completely my decision to have sex?
- How will I feel about it tomorrow?
- Will it bother me if I never see this person again after we have sex?
- Do I feel comfortable saying 'no' if I change my mind in the heat of the moment?
- Can I talk to this person about contraception?
- Do I feel safe with this person?
- Do I trust this person?
- Do I like this person?

Porn sex is not real-life sex

Pornography is a multibillion-dollar industry aimed at profits, not accurate or consensual sex education. Porn sex is a performance. It is a scripted fantasy that is highly edited and airbrushed and does not represent healthy sexual relationships.

Here are some differences between real life sex and porn sex:

- Porn sex is often done **to** a partner to dominate, punish or control. Real life sex is experienced **with** a partner to be intimate and affectionate.
- There is a lot more foreplay in real-life sex where outer parts of the body are touched. It takes women's bodies at least **20 minutes** to become aroused and ready for intercourse.
- Most women orgasm via the clitoris, not just via penetration which is often depicted in porn.

- The 'missionary position' is very common. There's no need to be a gymnastics champion and perform several positions in the bedroom.
- Couples cuddle after real-life sex.
- Real-life sex is consensual and involves verbal and non-verbal communication of consent between both people.
- Real-life sex can be awkward. You might fumble, fart and laugh!
- Sex is not a race to orgasm.
- Sex should be fun and enjoyable.

Overall, if you have any doubts, then you probably aren't ready. Talking it out and asking questions with someone you trust, such as an older sibling, parent, counsellor, teacher or friend, can be really helpful.

How do you ask someone to be your boyfriend/girlfriend?

You've been exclusively dating for a couple of months now. You've been texting and talking on a regular basis. You love being together. It feels like you are in a relationship, but neither of you have put a label on it. How do you bring up the 'what are we?' chat? Here are some things to consider…

Timing is everything

If you ask, 'what are we?' too soon, it might scare off your crush. But, if you wait too long, you could be wasting your time and become more emotionally attached when your crush might not feel the same way.

Overall, having the conversation earlier rather than later will save you a lot of heartache and investment in a relationship that's not going anywhere.

There is no set 'rule' on when to have 'the chat' – every relationship is different, but as a general guide, psychologists recommend waiting at least two months before asking someone to be in a relationship with you. You need time to get to know each other.

It's a nail-biting chat, but an important one

There is nothing more nerve-wracking than putting all your cards on the table and asking a crush if they want to take your 'situationship' to the next level. It's scary because 'what if they don't feel the same way?' Then at least you have an answer and can stop wondering and wasting more time. If this person is meant for you, then nothing will scare them off. Remind yourself that it's OK to ask for what you want.

Have the conversation face to face

I know these conversations are tough, but now is the time to be brave and avoid hiding behind your screen. Communication can get misinterpreted online. Plus, you don't want to have to wait for their response. You want to observe their body language and facial expression and read their response in the moment. Plus, if you want to be in a full-blown relationship with this person, then start practising mature conversations at the beginning.

How to bring it up

Here are some ideas of how you might want to start the conversation:

1. You can keep it light and start with some humour:

    'I know how much you love having "serious relationship chats", so I'm going to get the ball rolling by asking you if you have given any thought to where our relationship is going?'

    You can leave it there and wait for their response, or you can go further and state what you want:

    'I love spending time with you, and I'd love to make things official between us. Is that what you want, too?'

2. You can be cheeky:

    'I know how much you love spending time with me' or 'I know you can't seem to get enough of me lately, so do you want to make this thing between us official?'

3. Or you can be vulnerable:

    'You know how I've told you I find it hard to open up? Well, I'm going to be brave right now and tell you that I really like you, and I want to be your boyfriend/girlfriend. Is that what you want, too?'

If they say no

It will really sting if they tell you they aren't on the same page. You will feel disappointed, embarrassed, sad and potentially angry. You will feel 'not good enough' and confused. No matter how upset you feel, try your hardest to accept their decision graciously and kindly. They are allowed to want something different and the most important thing for you to preserve right now is your dignity. Respond with something along these lines:

   'Of course I'm disappointed that you don't feel the same way, but it's OK. I've loved spending time with you over the last couple of months and I wish you all the best.'

We will chat more about how to deal with rejection in the chapters on break-ups.

How do you turn your BFF into your lover?

Developing feelings for a BFF is normal. Attraction often grows after we get to know someone. But, transitioning from friends to lovers is not that straightforward and comes with the risk of losing your friend and your social group.

It's not impossible to turn your BFF into your boyfriend/girlfriend, but take time to evaluate the pros and cons of confessing your feelings because once it's out there, there is no turning back.

Here are some questions to ask yourself:

1. Are you both single?
2. Does your friend want to be in a relationship?

If the answer to these questions is 'no', then you might not want to risk it.

3. What are the chances that they have feelings for you, too?
4. How will it impact you if you say nothing?
5. If they don't feel the same way, can you realistically still be friends? How will it impact your friendship group?

Signs they might like you, too

We often show how we feel through our words and body language. Here are some things to consider:

- Has your friend sent you flirty texts?
- Do they lean into you closely when chatting?
- Do they maintain eye contact?
- Do they touch you whenever they get an opportunity?

These 'flirty signs' *might* indicate they feel the same way, but there are no guarantees until you ask them.

How do you tell them you want more than just friendship?

Choose a quiet location where you can talk without being interrupted.

There is no easy way to bring this up. It requires a lot of honesty and bravery. In person is always better because you will be able to deliver the message the way you intend and not risk miscommunication online.

Here is an example:

> 'You know how we normally tell each other everything? Well, there is something that I haven't told you lately because I'm scared it might ruin our friendship, but I need to be honest with you.
>
> 'We have been friends for a while now and I love spending time with you, but I've started developing feelings for you.
>
> 'You don't have to give me a response straight away as I know it's a lot to take in.
>
> 'It's OK if you don't feel the same. Our friendship is so important to me, and I hope me telling you this won't damage our relationship.'

Or keep it really short and direct:

> 'I love our friendship, but I want to take things to the next level. Would you be open to going on a date with me?'

Be kind to them and yourself if they don't feel the same way

There is a chance your feelings won't be reciprocated, which can be crushing. Respect their feelings. Don't be mad at them. They are allowed to feel what they feel. Take the high road and tell them it's OK and thank them for being honest. Decide what you want moving forward. Your friendship doesn't have to end. Hanging out with mutual friends in a group setting can help you get back to 'normal'.

But it also might be too hard to remain friends if you have strong feelings. It's going to feel a bit awkward between you for a while and you will naturally feel rejected. As disappointing as it is, be proud of yourself for speaking your truth. It's better to know how they feel rather than wasting more time and energy wondering.

Expressing how you feel can also lead to love! So, it's worth the risk if you think it might lead to something great.

Boundaries: behaviours you will and won't tolerate

Your house probably has a 'boundary fence' to mark where your property ends and your neighbour's property begins. If your neighbour decided to rip down your fence one day and build a pool in your backyard, you would have every right to tell them that this is not OK. Boundaries are like metaphorical fences; they are a line that represents behaviours we are comfortable with and behaviours we are not comfortable with. They help us to take care of the 'environments' of our lives.

When we don't have boundaries, it's like having no fence. No one knows your limits or where the edge of your property ends. This means that anyone can walk all over your lawn, pick your flowers or park their car in your driveway. No boundaries can cause chaos and confusion because no one knows where they stand. It can also leave you feeling resentful and manipulated because people can walk all over you.

What does having no boundaries look like?

- Your date says they will meet you at the café at 10am and they arrive at 11am. You wait and have to cancel plans to see your friends in the afternoon. When they arrive, they make a poor excuse. You smile and say, 'no worries'.

- Your love interest hasn't replied to your last message for 24 hours. As soon as they reply, you write back straight away with lots of emoji kisses.

- Your date contacts you on Friday afternoon and asks if you want to catch up in a couple of hours. You already had movie plans with your friends but ditch them to see your new lover.

- Your love interest tells you they are meeting up with an ex or sends flirty messages to boys/girls you have never met, and you don't ask any questions.

- You start kissing your date and he puts his hand up your shirt. This makes you uncomfortable. You quietly say, 'I don't know if we should do this' and he says, 'it's OK' and continues to touch you. You let him, until you make an excuse to leave.

- Your lover asks you to send a nude photo. You don't really want to but send one anyway.

What does having healthy boundaries look like?

- You can say 'no' when something doesn't align to your values or makes you feel uncomfortable.
- You understand your responsibilities (for example, you are responsible for how you treat others, but you are not responsible for other people's happiness or how they treat you).
- You are assertive. You can be direct and honest with someone without being rude or mean.
- You are flexible without being too rigid in your thoughts and actions.
- You can be vulnerable and share personal information without over- or undersharing.

Journal Time

What behaviours are you willing and not willing to accept?

Write a list of what makes you feel comfortable or uncomfortable when it comes to sexual behaviour, the way someone speaks to you, treats you and their values and morals.

Behaviours that make me feel comfortable	Behaviours that make me feel uncomfortable	What will you do or say if someone makes you feel uncomfortable?

Ghosting

Ghosting occurs when someone cuts off all contact with you and vanishes into thin air. It can happen after you have been on a few dates, or it can happen after a few text exchanges or when someone unfollows or blocks you on social media. There are two reasons people may ghost: they have lost interest and don't have the maturity to communicate their feelings and are scared about how you might respond, or there might be someone else on the scene.

Ghosting can sting because it leaves you hanging and wondering. The best way to handle being ghosted is to get on with your life and not send that person any more messages. They don't deserve your precious time or energy. No answer is your answer. Next!

CHAPTER 7

How to be in a relationship

How to strengthen your connection

Look after what you value

Being in a relationship with someone you trust, respect and love can be the best feeling in the world. But just because you have made it through the 'dating stage' and are no longer feeling confused about your 'situationship' doesn't mean it's time to slide into your trackies, step into your UGG boots and crawl into the 'relationship cave' and hibernate.

Like anything valuable in life, if we want to maintain its value, we have to look after it. A Tiffany bracelet will tarnish if it's not polished, an Apple Watch will malfunction if we don't update the settings regularly, a Chanel handbag might crack if we don't condition the leather, and a BMW will break down if we don't get it serviced.

A relationship will also tarnish, malfunction, crack and break down if we don't look after it properly.

Tips on how to strengthen your relationship

1. Give your partner more positive praise than criticism

Conflict is going to occur in all your relationships. You might argue over one of you being late all the time or one of you staying in contact with an ex or not spending enough time with your friends. Conflict is inevitable.

One of the world's leading relationship researchers, John Gottman, has discovered that for every negative interaction we have with our partner, we need to balance this with five positive interactions.

Negative interactions look like:
- Raising your voice
- Rolling your eyes
- Ignoring
- Criticising ('you never listen to me', 'you're always on your phone')
- Being defensive ('that's not true; I do listen to you! You're just being overly sensitive')
- Not being willing to apologise
- Not listening, interrupting
- Rejecting your partner when they make an effort to connect with you (for example, your partner shares a funny video and you ignore it)

Positive interactions look like:
- Telling your partner what you love about them regularly
- Saying 'thank you' frequently
- Showing affection (holding hands, saying 'I love you')
- Performing acts of kindness to make their life easier
- Listening

- Planning fun activities to do together
- Responding positively when your partner tries to connect with you (for example, if they ask, 'how was your day?' instead of saying, 'fine', give them some more detail)
- Validating their feelings when they are upset (for example, 'it makes sense you feel like that', 'I would feel disappointed, too', 'I understand where you are coming from')

The goal is to have more positive interactions that will keep your relationship in a positive emotional state. Gottman suggests that you should try and do 'small things often'. So, the next time you have an argument, it won't damage the relationship because you have buffered it with all your positive interactions.

2. Be a 'joy multiplier'

Imagine that your partner tells you some good news; they got a new job, they aced an exam or they received a compliment from a teacher.

How do you respond when they share their good news?

a. **Conversation killer:** Do you continue doing what you are doing (for example, texting, watching television) and say 'well done' in an unexcited tone, implying you're not really listening?

b. **Conversation hijacker:** Do you completely ignore them and leave the room? Or hijack the conversation and make it all about you? 'You won't believe the day I've had!'

c. **Joy thief:** Do you put your partner down by telling them you are surprised by their good news and point out their flaws and all the things that will go wrong and all the disadvantages of their good news?

d. **Joy multiplier:** Do you smile and say 'congratulations!' in an excited tone; stop whatever you are doing and give them your full attention; ask questions and hug; or celebrate their good news by going out to lunch?

Being a 'joy multiplier' is the best way to respond to someone's good news because, by asking questions, hugging, giving eye contact and celebrating, you are making their good news last, which makes their positive emotions bigger and last longer, too. You are helping your loved one to relive and savour the positive feelings that came from their good news again. You are showing that you care and understand the importance of their good news, which shows you also understand and care about your relationship (Gable & Reis, 2010).

So, the next time your special someone chooses you to share their good news with, make it count and make it last!

3. Ask for what you need – making a DEAL

Have you ever struggled to ask for what you need? You might find it difficult to ask your partner to stop 'hearting' their ex's posts on Instagram; or you need them to be more affectionate with you in front of their friends; or you need them to be a better listener; or you need them to respond more promptly to your messages.

There are two main reasons we struggle to ask for what we need:

1. Fear – we are too scared (what if they break up with us?!)
2. We don't know how

Fear

Most people are afraid to speak up for themselves because humans worry about 'getting kicked out of the group'. Many people stay silent because they are afraid that speaking their mind will destroy their relationships. They fear that the other person won't like them or will get mad at them or want revenge. But when we stay silent, we aren't being our true selves and we will feel disempowered, resentful and our confidence will be crushed. If your partner isn't open to at least trying to accommodate your needs (if they are reasonable), then they might not be 'your person'.

We don't know how

The other reason we stay silent is because we don't know how to start the conversation. We don't know the words to say. We don't know how to express our feelings and emotions confidently.

How to ask for what you need

Here is a model to help you ask for what you need:

Describe	Describe the problem objectively
Express	Express how it made you feel
Ask	Ask for what you need
List	List the improvements the change will make

Adapted from DBT Therapy

Here are two examples of what this might look like in action:

My girlfriend doesn't trust me. I want her to stop being so clingy and checking up on me all the time.

Describe	On Friday night at the party, I bumped into some of my female friends from school and you didn't leave my side all night. When we get home, I caught you checking my phone.
Express	This made me feel angry and disrespected.
Ask	I'd appreciate it if you would trust me by giving me space when we are socialising and not go behind my back and check my phone.
List	If you do that, then I will want to spend more time with you and share things more openly rather than keep things to myself because I'm worried you will take it the wrong way.

You can use this model in any relationship. Here is an example of how it could be used in a friendship:

I don't like the way my friend speaks to me. I want her to stop being mean.

Describe	On Tuesday we were in my room looking at old photos with our friends and you said, 'that was in Sarah's fat era' and everyone laughed.
Express	This made me feel embarrassed and humiliated.
Ask	I'd appreciate it if you would stop putting me down and making fun of my weight.
List	If you do that, then I'll be more open to sharing stuff with you and hanging out more often.

You might not get what you want

Just because you have the confidence to ask for what you want, you are not guaranteed to get it! We can't control the outcome. We can't control how others will respond to our requests. But at least we have the courage to express our needs and not allow others to walk all over us. And if the person doesn't agree to make a change that's really impacting you, then perhaps they are not worth having around.

PART THREE
Heartbreak and rejection

CHAPTER 8

How to deliver and handle a break-up

Break up or make up?

Making a decision to stay in or leave a relationship can be difficult, especially if your partner hasn't really done anything wrong. Sometimes you just stop 'clicking' or sometimes it might be more clearcut if they cheated on you. Here are some questions to help you make the right decision for you:

✏ Journal Time

How has your boyfriend/girlfriend <u>negatively</u> affected these parts of your life? (You might want to add them to the table over the page.)

Family

Friends

Goals

Self-esteem

School (your grades and attendance)

Self-confidence

Physical health

Mental health

Hobbies

Reasons I should go	Reasons I should stay

- Is there a way to work through some of the 'reasons to go'? And do you *want* to work through them?
- Have you told your partner how you feel and given them a chance to work through problems with you together?
- Will you regret breaking up?

How do you break up with your partner?

1. Practise what you want to say

If you have decided your relationship is definitely over, then the next step is to get clear on the reasons you want to break up. Write them down. Practise what you are going to say so you can feel confident when you say it.

2. Break up face to face

Always break up in person and don't do it over social media (unless you think your partner might hurt you or if they have cheated on you). It's the respectful thing to do. Your partner deserves a face-to-face break-up. While you may think it's hard to break the news, remember that your partner is going to find this a lot harder.

3. Only break up over text when...

If you have been dating for a short time (a few dates, a couple of weeks or a month or two), then it's reasonable to send a text to say, 'I've enjoyed hanging out with you, but I'm not really feeling a connection' or, 'I've loved spending time with you, but if we were to see each other again it would be as friends, as I'm not feeling a romantic connection with you'.

4. Suggestions on what you might say

If you have been together for three months or more, here are some suggestions of what to say in person:

Tell them what you appreciate and value about your time together

- 'I've loved spending time with you and getting to know you.'
- 'I'm so thankful for all the fun times we have had together.'

Explain what's not working and why you want to end it

- 'I've been doing a lot of thinking, and I think it's best we end our relationship because...
- 'I'm not ready to fully commit to you and be in a serious relationship and I don't want to waste your time.'
- 'You cheated on me and I can't get over that.'
- 'I think we are on different pages and want different things.'
- 'I can't give you what you want right now.'
- 'It doesn't feel right anymore. We spend more time arguing than having fun.'

Empathise with how much this is going to hurt

- 'I don't want to hurt you.'
- 'I'm sorry if this hurts.'
- 'I know this is not easy to hear.'

Explain the importance of honesty and respect

- 'I really care about you and respect you, which is why I want to be honest about my feelings.'

Avoid blame

- 'There isn't anything specific you did or didn't do. I think you are a wonderful person, but just not "my person" and you deserve to be happy.'

Offer support and space

- 'I'm here if you want to talk further, but I also understand if you need some time and space. I'll respect whatever you need to process this.'

Be prepared for your partner to be upset. Listen to what they want to say and try to answer their questions as best you can.

Overall, make sure you are honest, kind and respectful.

How do you respond when someone breaks up with you?

Nothing will prepare you for the moment someone breaks up with you. It's awful. But the most important thing you want to walk away with is your dignity intact. Here is how you can do that:

1. Take deep breaths and plant your feet into the ground to try to remain calm and grounded. You can lose your s**t by screaming and swearing once they leave, but do everything you can to keep your cool throughout the conversation. It's completely OK and normal if you cry.

2. Ask them as many questions as you need, to try to understand their reasons for wanting to end things.

3. Tell them how you feel and what you think, but don't insult or blame them. This is hard when you are feeling angry and rejected, but it doesn't achieve anything and makes you look like 'the crazy person'. If you feel like you are going to lash out, then ask if you can continue the conversation another time.

4. Don't beg them to stay. You are not needy, and you are not desperate. If someone doesn't want your 'fabulous self' in their life, then show them the door! They don't deserve another moment of your precious time and energy.

5. Try to end on a good note. Tell them all the things you are grateful for and all the things you will miss about being with them, then close the door firmly behind you. Don't ask them to call you or text you and don't ask to see them again. It will only prolong your recovery.

Why it's important to remain cool and calm during a break-up chat

- It shows confidence and demonstrates to your ex you can survive without them.
- It shows you have good self-control; you can handle yourself during stressful moments when you are a hurting.
- It will make you feel strong rather than weak and pathetic.
- It will surprise your ex who might assume you will lose your bananas. It will show them you don't need them, and you are going to be OK without them, which can sometimes cause them to second-guess their decision.
- If you can end on a good note, you will earn your ex's respect and give them nothing nasty to say about you.
- You won't feel ashamed or regret your actions afterwards. Break-ups strip us of our confidence, but if you walk away with your dignity intact, you will feel proud of yourself for keeping your cool and that will help you to start rebuilding your confidence again.

If you are still at school with your ex

- Find different routes to get around school to avoid bumping into them.
- Avoid going to places where you know your ex hangs out.
- Don't feel like you have to stop and chat if you run into them. Smile and keep moving. You don't owe them anything.
- Sit in the front row if you share a class with them so you don't have to look at them.
- Accept that it's going to be awkward when you see each other no matter what. Make peace with that and know it's not going to last.

What if you have 'break-up regret'?

Reasons you might have 'break-up regret' include:

- You miss them.
- Dating can be hard.
- With time and space you forget their bad qualities and begin to idolise them and only remember their 'highlight reel'.
- You had a 'reactive break-up'. You broke up impulsively in the 'heat of the moment' rather than making an intentional conscious decision.

What to do if you have 'break-up regret' or if your ex comes back?

- Slow down. Sit with your discomfort. It's normal to grieve the end of a relationship.
- Ask yourself the following questions to work out if you want to get back together:
    1. Did my ex bring out the best in me?
    2. Did my ex want the best for me?
    3. Did we share the same values and long-term goals?
    4. What would our relationship look like now if we got back together?
- If you end up contacting your ex, be prepared that they may have moved on.

Why do breaks-up hurt so much? What happens in our brains?

Love withdrawal

Did you know that studies have shown that the pain we feel during a break-up lights up the same parts of the brain as a drug user when they are looking for a 'fix'? Our brain is literally in withdrawal after a break-up. This is because when we are in love our bodies are constantly making feel-good hormones called oxytocin and dopamine. When we are no longer with our partner these hormones suddenly stop, so the 'withdrawal' we feel is very difficult to process.

When we experience rejection, our brain is still in love. We are still looking for the 'dopamine hit' we get from a cuddle, a text or a chat with our partner.

It takes time to learn to live without this 'hit'. When we make contact with our ex, go through old messages or photos, or fixate on their social media, we activate those old neural pathways. This only makes you hold on to your ex. As painful as cutting all contact with your ex can be, it allows these old neural pathways in your brain to weaken and eventually be replaced by new pathways.

CHAPTER 9

How to cope after a break-up

Break-ups feel similar to grieving a death because your ex is no longer in your life. Grief is a natural and important human emotion; it is the process of working through a broken heart.

Unlike healing a broken arm which can take six weeks, healing from a break-up is not quick or straightforward.

Researchers tell us that there are certain stages that we go through when we are grieving the loss of someone, but we don't always move through them in a straightforward fashion. There will be days when you start to feel better and don't think about your ex as much, only to find yourself struggling to get out of bed again the next day or stalking them on social media. I think the diagram below illustrates what the grief process can look like.

Grief

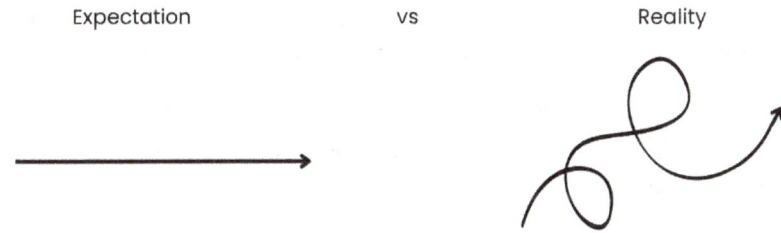

Expectation   vs   Reality

Shock: *This can't be happening*

Your body often goes into shock after someone breaks up with you because your body sees your separation as a threat. Shock is a defence response; it helps to conserve blood flow to your vital organs such as your brain, heart and lungs.

Physical symptoms of shock:

Numbness

Dizziness

Faster heartrate

Shortness of breath

Chest pain

Headaches

Tense muscles

Vomiting

Stress hormones also divert blood away from our digestive system which can cause stomach aches and loss of appetite.

You may feel as though you are falling apart, but everything you are feeling is completely normal. Your body is just reacting to all the stress that is flooding your body.

Coping strategies

1. *Talk to someone*

Calm your nervous system by finding someone who is grounded, good at listening and can support you without judgement.

Tell your 'support person' what you need from them: 'I don't need your advice or for you to rant about my ex, I just need you to listen so I can process what has happened.'

2. *Don't bottle up your feelings*

If we don't feel our emotions and process them by crying, talking, exercising, writing, etc., they will build up inside us and eventually explode in destructive ways that can impact other relationships. 'There is no way out but through.' Feel your feelings and keep reminding yourself that 'this too shall pass'.

Denial: *Everything is fine*

The day after your break-up you might think 'this can't be real' or 'they are just upset, they will call me tomorrow'. You might tell yourself that 'everything will be fine; once I talk to my ex again, we will sort it out'.

Our brain often goes into 'denial' when we hear unwanted news. It's our brain's defence system that helps to dull the pain. Denial gives our hearts time to process the news and gradually adjust to our new situation.

Denial looks like:

♦ Texting or calling your ex or hoping they will contact you

♦ Refusing to believe that this is happening to you

♦ Daydreaming about them showing up at your door wanting to get back together

Contacting your ex will keep you stuck in the denial stage and make the pain worse. Imagine if you held on to a heavy weight for too long. It would hurt. If you let it go, the pain will go away. The sooner you can let go and accept that you are no longer together and there is nothing you can do to change the past, the sooner you can start recovering.

Coping strategies

1. *Don't contact your ex*

Your ex is like an addictive drug. The more you stay in touch with them, the more they stay in your 'system', and it becomes impossible to 'break the habit'.

Applying the 'no contact rule' will allow you to create some space so you can focus on yourself and begin the healing process. The other reason no contact is important is because we can be in a very emotional and unstable state after a break-up. The last thing we want is to say or do something we will later regret. Instead of picking up the phone to call them, call a friend, go for a walk or pick up a pen and write about how you are feeling.

✏ Journal Time

2. *Reflect on your needs*

We tend to romanticise our relationship when it ends. But were all your needs really met? Circle which of the following needs are important to you in a relationship:

Affection	Respect	Words of affirmation	Trust	Security
Loyalty	Listening		Humour	Commitment
Honest communication	Organisation and planning	Family values	Quality time	Intellectual connection
		Spontaneity	Ability to reflect	
Physical connection	Creativity	Kindness		Freedom

Reflect on your needs above by answering the questions below:

What needs were met in your relationship?	What needs were not met?

3. *Avoid bargaining by focusing on your ex's negative qualities*

Bargaining involves debate and going 'back and forth' to come up with an agreement.

When the loneliness and pain of missing an ex becomes unbearable, we start thinking 'what could I have done differently?' or 'if only I...' We might find reasons to bump into them or contact them and try to 'bargain' with them by making a promise to change in the hope of getting them back.

The reason we bargain is to try to gain some control over an uncontrollable situation. Plus, we want to put ourselves out of misery because break-ups are incredibly painful.

Bargaining to get your ex back will only make your emotional distress bigger and last longer. Instead, focus your energy on your ex's negative qualities:

- Write a list of your ex's negative qualities on your phone and look at this list every time you want to make contact.
- Write a response to this question: were there 'red flags' at the start of your relationship that you ignored?
- What didn't feel right when you were with your ex?

4. *Create a distraction plan*

When you start to crave your ex, remind yourself that the craving will only last 20–30 minutes. Sometimes the wait can feel like it will never end! But the longing for them will lessen. Write a list of things you can do to distract yourself when the cravings come, for example:

- Call a friend.
- Go for a walk.
- Watch a 30-minute show.
- Do an online exercise class.
- Look at your list of your ex's negative qualities.

Depression: *Life sucks*

The pain and stress caused by a break-up can also lead us to feeling depressed. Here are signs that you might be depressed:

- Feeling sad and anxious most of the time
- Difficulty sleeping
- Loss of interest in activities you used to love
- Feeling tired and having no energy
- Difficulty focusing and finishing tasks
- Feeling angry or irritable
- Thinking about death, suicide or self-harm

Coping strategies

1. *Feel your emotions, but don't 'add on' or run away from them*

<u>Feeling your emotions</u> means to sit with them, allow them to wash over you, be present with them, accept them and let them pass.

- Breathe in for four counts and out for eight.
- Talk about your feelings to friends, family or a professional.
- Write about your feelings.
- Exercise.

<u>Adding on to your emotions</u> means telling yourself stories that aren't necessarily true. For example, if you are feeling sad, you might add on to this emotion by saying:

'I'm never going to find someone.'

'They dumped me because I'm not attractive.'

'My life is over.'

'My friends will think it was my fault.'

Running away from your emotions means to avoid, push away and not let yourself feel your emotions. Try to avoid the following...

Avoiding our emotions looks like numbing the pain by:

- Taking drugs
- Drinking alcohol
- Eating poorly
- Having casual sex with different people

Less destructive behaviours look like:

- Scrolling endlessly on social media
- Watching Netflix for weeks
- Throwing yourself into work or study

2. *Set 'thought boundaries'*

You're more likely to get depressed when you think about something repeatedly. If you find your sadness spiralling (can't get out of bed, can't stop crying), set a timer for how long you are going to feel sad (20–30 minutes), then change your state – have a cold shower, go for a walk, call a friend, dance around to some music you love, write three things you are grateful for. Repeat this every day until you start to feel better.

Anger: *What a jerk!*

I understand that you may want to go and punch your ex in the face, slam them on social media or smash their bedroom windows, but lashing out isn't going to make you feel better in the long run. It's more likely to make you feel regret and embarrassed once you start to think more clearly again. You might also direct your anger at yourself and blame yourself for the break-up, which will only make you feel worse.

Coping strategies

1. *Move your body*

Anger can be helpful when we process it in a healthy way. Instead of allowing anger to stay stuck in your body, move it by exercising. Go for a run or walk, sign up to a boxing or high-intensity interval class. Exercise is a great way of channelling your anger and helping you to feel in control. Not only does it make you feel good and reduces your depression, it will also make you look hot, which is the perfect revenge on your ex.

2. *Let it out*

Sometimes when we are angry, we hold it in our throats, making it feel tight and constricted. Another way of getting the anger out of our body is through our voice while we are moving. The next time you go for a run or a walk or do some star jumps, try howling, screaming or sighing out loud making an *ahhhhhhhh* sound. You can also do this underwater. Take some deep breaths when you are done and see if you feel any lighter.

Acceptance: *Everything is going to be OK*

It can take months of crying and obsessing over your ex to reach this stage. Break-ups require a lot of patience and self-kindness. But if you have allowed yourself to feel your feelings and process them, one day you will wake up and your heart will feel lighter; you will have made peace with your relationship being over, and the resentment you once held towards your ex won't seem as strong.

In saying this, it's normal to have moments where you still feel sad or miss your ex. But the difference this time is that the sadness doesn't consume and take control over you. You can let it pass through you more easily.

Just because you are feeling better doesn't mean 'the work' stops here. It's important to reflect back on what you have learnt and continue your self-care rituals, so you are better able to cope the next time you have a setback.

✎ Journal Time

What did you learn?

In your journal answer these questions:

- What did this break-up teach you about yourself?
- What are you most proud of when you look back at your heartbreak journey? Why?
- What will you do differently in the next relationship?
- What are some self-care rituals you want to continue practising? How can you ensure they remain part of your daily routine?

Are you ready to start dating again?

Some people rush into dating or hooking up with someone soon after a break-up to try and numb the pain, but this will only prolong your healing. Read the statements in the below table to see if you're ready to start dating again.

You are ready to date again if...	You are not ready to date again if...
• Seeing your ex with someone new IRL or on social media might sting but won't completely 'undo' you • You are excited by the thought of meeting new people • You are ready to have some fun • You won't fall apart if someone ghosts you • Your expectations are realistic, you understand that dating take practise and the first person who asks you out might not turn into a long-term relationship • You can have a conversation where you don't bring up your ex	• You want to distract and avoid your feelings • You start seeing someone new to get back at your ex or make them jealous • You are still in the 'shock' or 'denial' phase of the break-up • Seeing your ex with someone new will 'undo' you • You need validation and someone to boost your confidence • You are trying to get your ex back

Conclusion

In her song 'Lover', Taylor Swift sings:

Can I go where you go?
Can we always be this close forever and ever?

Being in love is the best feeling in the world, but love can also cause us great pain and confusion. It can cause us to lose our confidence, our trust and our way.

Your ability to get through the hardships of love lies in your resilience: how you cope and bounce back when you are ghosted, when your partner betrays you or when you are dumped.

You build this resilience by practising all the lessons in Chapter 1. Nothing in this book will work if you haven't worked on loving yourself first.

You can't control when 'your person' is going to magically swoop you off your feet, nor can you control if they are going to break your heart. The only thing you can control is learning how to love yourself and having a solid understanding of who you are and what you want.

You are also in control of *how* you love others and *who* you do and don't let into your life. So, instead of worrying about what's going to happen or what's not going to happen in the future, invest your energy into loving *you* and being the very best person you can be. Treat your confidence like a part-time job and work on building it every single day.

In the words of Lizzo:

True love finally happens when you by yourself...
'Cause [you are your] own soulmate (Yeah, yeah)
[you] know how to love [yourself]...
Look up in the mirror like 'Damn, [I'm] the one'

References

Apostolou, M., & Christoforou, C. (2022). What Makes Single Life Attractive: An Explorative Examination of the Advantages of Singlehood. *Evolutionary Psychological Science, 8*(4), 403-412.

Buunk, A.P., & Gibbons, F.X. (2006). Social comparison orientation: A new perspective on those who do and those who don't compare with others. *Social Comparison and Social Psychology: Understanding cognition, intergroup relations and culture,* 15-32.

Fisher, H.E., Brown, L.L., Aron, A., Strong, G., & Mashek, D. (2010). Reward, addiction, and emotion regulation systems associated with rejection in love. *Journal of Neurophysiology; 104*(1):51-60.

Fredrickson, B.L. (2014). *Love 2.0: Creating Happiness and Health in Moments of Connection.* Penguin Group.

Gable, S.L., & Reis, H.T. (2010). Good news! Capitalizing on positive events in an interpersonal context. In M.P. Zanna (Ed.), *Advances in experimental social psychology,* Vol. 42, pp. 195-257. Academic Press.

Gottman, J. (1999). *The Seven Principles for Making a Marriage Work.* Harmony.

Nakamura, J., & Csikszentmihalyi, M. (2002). The Concept of Flow. *Handbook of Positive Psychology,* 89-105.

Niemiec, R.M. (2017). *Character Strengths Interventions: A Field Guide for Practitioners.* Hogrefe Publishing.

Park, J., Ayduk, Ö., & Kross, E. (2016). Stepping back to move forward: Expressive writing promotes self-distancing. *Emotion, 16*(3), 349-64.

Pennebaker, J.W., & Beall, S.K. (1986). Confronting a traumatic event: Toward an understanding of inhibition and disease. *Journal of Abnormal Psychology*, 95(3), 274–281.

Sheldon, K.M., & Lyubomirsky, S. (2006). How to increase and sustain positive emotion: The effects of expressing gratitude and visualizing best possible selves. *The Journal of Positive Psychology*, 1(2), 73–82.

Walker, M. (2018). *Why We Sleep: Unlocking the Power of Sleep and Dreams.* Scribner Book Company.

Winch, G. (2018). *How to fix a broken heart.* Simon & Schuster/TED.

Young, B. (2017). The Impact of Timing of Pornography Exposure on Mental Health, Life Satisfaction, and Sexual Behavior. *Theses and Dissertations.* 6727. https://scholarsarchive.byu.edu/etd/6727

www.ingramcontent.com/pod-product-compliance
Lightning Source LLC
Chambersburg PA
CBHW052111070526
44584CB00017B/2437